LIVING WITH YOUR
FEELINGS

Living With Your Feelings

Barry Bailey

ABINGDON   NASHVILLE

LIVING WITH YOUR FEELINGS

Library of Congress Catologing in Publication Data

Bailey, Barry, 1926–
  Living with your feelings.
  1. Methodist Church—Sermons.   2. Sermons,
American. I. Title.
BX8333.B24L58   252'.07   79-27889
ISBN 0-687-22380-6

Scripture quotations, unless otherwise noted, are from
the Revised Standard Version of the Bible, copyrighted
1946, 1952, © 1971, 1973 by the Division of Christian
Education of the National Council of the Churches of
Christ in the U.S.A.

Book Design and Illustrations by
Laura B. Wooten

MANUFACTURED BY THE PARTHENON PRESS AT
NASHVILLE, TENNESSEE, UNITED STATES OF AMERICA

*This book is dedicated to
the congregation
of
First United Methodist Church
Fort Worth, Texas
on the fiftieth anniversary
of their sanctuary*

CONTENTS

LIVING WITH YOUR
FEELINGS

Building On Failure

CHAPTER I

And as Peter was below in the courtyard, one of the maids of the high priest came; and seeing Peter warming himself, she looked at him, and said, "You also were with the Nazarene, Jesus." But he denied it, saying, "I neither know nor understand what you mean." And he went out into the gateway. And the maid saw him, and began again to say to the bystanders, "This man is one of them." But again he denied it. And after a little while again the bystanders said to Peter, "Certainly you are one of them; for you are a Galilean." But he began to invoke a curse on himself and to swear, "I do not know this man of whom you speak." And immediately the cock crowed a second time. And Peter remembered how Jesus had said to him, "Before the cock crows twice, you will deny me three times." And he broke down and wept.

—*Mark 14:66-72*

One of the most significant aspects of the Bible is its honesty; it deals with the genuine. Regrettably, it is often introduced to us as a religious book, and we fail to grasp its authenticity. The Bible is not a promise of the religious success that *follows* faith, but the candid history of people struggling *for* faith.

With this quality of the Bible in mind, let us look at Simon Peter's story. On the last night of Jesus' life on earth, Simon Peter was there. He was following Jesus at a careful distance, though to his eternal credit, Simon Peter *was* present—most of Jesus' other disciples were not. While they were standing beside a fire, a young woman turned to Peter and said, "You're one of his disciples, aren't you?" And Peter replied, "I don't know what you mean." Someone else said, "You are one of his disciples. You're a follower of that man!" And again Simon Peter said, "I don't know him!" Then, the third time it happened, Simon was angry and lashed back with an oath, "I don't even know what you are talking about. I don't know him at all." And at that moment, the cock began to crow. In Luke's account, Jesus then turned and looked at Simon Peter, who remembered Jesus' prediction about the denial, and Simon Peter went away and wept bitterly.

Doesn't that story describe some characteristics similar to our own? We pride ourselves on our loyalty and steadfastness. We are boastful and often appear very sure of ourselves. But beneath all that, we can be rather disgusting people. We are weak; we can be egotistical and sinful. Often, we prove not to be dependable at all. We behave as Simon Peter did.

Peter's story does not stop here, however. A few weeks after his denial of Christ, this same man, Simon Peter, stood up to preach a sermon. Surely, he was aware that someone would remember his earlier failure and say, "Who are you to speak to us? Why, you denied him. Three times you said you didn't even know who Jesus was, and now you're trying to preach!" But I don't think that denouncement would have threatened Peter; he did not try to disregard that failure in his life. He never forgot it, we can be sure—he did not try to make a new beginning by wiping the slate clean. He was strong because he knew who he was. I think Peter would look us squarely in the eye and he would say, "That's right. I denied him. Yet now I'm asking you to follow him, so that you can see what he can make of your life." That is not just great preaching; that is the heroic substance from which life is made!

Yet, look how artificial we are! When we have problems, we try to put them in the past in order to make a fresh start. It is very much like the way most of us make New Year's resolutions; we have grown up with the idea of wiping the slate clean and starting over again. In our society and in our religion we cry, "Start all over again. Let us have a fresh beginning!" and we pretend that we did not do what we have done.

However, we are haunted by this falseness because we are not dealing with reality. We cannot really start over, for we are who we are. Even if we could literally begin again, we would not recognize ourselves. If we got rid of all our weaknesses, nobody would know us. We would be total strangers to ourselves and to one another.

There is a far better approach than starting over again. And that is building on what we already are—the good traits and the bad, our strengths and our weaknesses.

Let us look at several aspects of starting where we are. For many of us, one impediment to doing so is that we major in our disappointments. Some people dramatize their weaknesses and cling to their failures. What if Simon Peter had talked only about his denial of Jesus? Suppose that every time he stood up to preach he had told that same story. Who would not have grown tired of it? And of him! We can weep with someone only so long—we run out of Kleenex after a while. If Peter had preached in that way, he would not have grown, and his audience would have dwindled. But there are some of us who are happy only when we are sad; we feel secure only when we are lost. We are determined to be more miserable than anyone else. We become caught in our failures.

Martin Luther was one of the great leaders of the church in the sixteenth century and is credited with being a founder of the Protestant Reformation. As a young Catholic priest, and before he was disassociated from the church he loved so much, Luther not only went to confession every day, he would have gone almost every hour.

On most nights, Luther slept well, but he felt guilty about it, thinking, "Here am I, sinful as I am, having a good night's sleep." So he would confess that. One day the older priest to whom Luther went for confession said to him, "Martin, either find a new sin and commit it, or quit coming to see me!"

I love that story, because it describes us as Christians. We play that one note, "O God, have mercy upon me!" and we weep and wail. We have read the text that tells us that God is supposed to have mercy upon us, so we go about dripping despair.

Another barrier some of us encounter in starting where we are, is that we rationalize our actions so effectively that we do not realize that we ever do anything wrong. Generally insensitive to our own sins, we reason that those "little" wrong things we do are not serious. But if it is dangerous to cling to our wrongdoings, it is just as dangerous to be so well defended against our sins that we are unaware of them. We can be so convinced that we are good; the fact that we do not commit certain great sins gives us a false security, and we conclude that we never do anything wrong.

Jesus once turned to some people who were better than we will ever be at keeping the Law and said, in effect, "Quite frankly, the prostitutes are going to get into heaven ahead of you. At least they know what to confess. They know where their sin is." Goodness can so blind us that we think, "O God, it's so marvelous for you to have me in your presence." If we are not aware of any of our wrongdoings, we will never find our true selves.

There is a third pitfall that is especially prevalent among those of us in the church. Our problem is that we play the religious game; we want to be *so* religious. Jesus did not say, "Come, follow me and be religious." Rather, he asked us to find the truth. There is a difference! Did it ever occur to us that some of our efforts to be religious can make us blind to the truth? Those efforts are our attempts to use religion for our own ends by being manipulative or trying to control God. For instance, at a football game, each team may pray to win. According to some popular religions, both teams come onto the field, and the one that prays the best, wins. God does not have anything to do with such prayer. God answers prayer, but not like that—that is not how prayer works!

Recently, I read about a young man who played football for Notre Dame. He was very intelligent and planned to go into medicine. He was "turned on" to Jesus because Notre Dame had won a number of football games and that had made him feel much closer to Christ. That was his theology. Can't we see through that? Should we thank God that he was going to go out and "sack 'em for the Savior . . . jab 'em for Jesus . . . martinize them for the Messiah"? Surely the Lord is more concerned about other issues. But how well we manage to play the religious game, like that young man! In doing so, we hide our failures and responsibilities from ourselves; we try to manipulate God and ourselves.

The manipulative religious game does not work. Simon Peter *could* have been religious in that sense. But notice how honest the New Testament is. It does not play down what Peter did, nor does Peter himself minimize his actions. We are not told that he was right or that he could start over by pretending that he did not deny Jesus. Three times Peter had said, "I don't even know who this Jesus is," and he had cursed. How would we like to have that reported about us in the newspaper, let alone in the New Testament!

When Jesus turned and looked at Simon Peter, we know what happened. Peter did exactly what we must do at times—he wept bitterly. That is better than wiping the slate clean and starting over again. That is *better* than a new beginning. God worked with Peter where he was, not through pretending to be where he was not. And because of that, Peter moved beyond his existing condition. Peter suddenly realized who he was. Until then he had been bluffing, playing a religious game, for he had said, in effect, "O Lord, don't tell me I am going to deny you. Look how good I am!" In that denial and in the aftermath, the whole Simon Peter was brought into focus. He would never forget who he was, and that was his power.

From the story of Peter we learn the power of starting where we are, and out of this knowledge, we can conclude three things. First, *we ought to stop running from ourselves.* Who are we trying to impress? People who know us and like us for what we are, already see us more clearly than we want them to. Who are we trying to fool? Simon Peter could have stood up each time he preached and said, "I want you to know how much I love Jesus." But that is not how he went about it—he told his story and let people see that the gospel can take a man who is weak and make him a rock. Simon began to reveal who he was—to himself, and to other people.

So let us stop running from ourselves. If you are an alcoholic, admit it! You do not have to drink. If you have lied, you do not have to deny it to stop doing it. If you have hurt others, if you have been weak and self-destructive, do not lie about it. If any of us ever change, it will not be because we have pretended we did not do wrong. If we ever change for the better, it will be because we have had the audacity to recognize our weakness and to see who we are.

We do not have innocent politics here in Texas, but for flamboyant politics that almost defy description, look at Louisiana! When I lived in Louisiana there was a governor who was not known for his polish, and from the standpoint of politics, he was unpredictable. He did a number of bizarre things, and his wife had him placed in a mental institution. That governor *announced* that his wife had placed him in the institution. Nothing hidden there! Further, the man declared that he was going to run for Congress. In almost any other state in the nation, it would have been all over for him, but not in Louisiana.

The governor was released from the institution, and at a news conference, he held up his discharge papers and said, "I'm sane and I can prove it. Those other rascals who are running for this office are afraid to be committed because they're not so sure they can get out!" Believe it or not, that man was elected to the congressional seat.

I am not trying to teach a course in political science, but merely pointing out that that politician was smart. He could have lied. He could have said that he had been away for a little rest. But then he would not have been elected, even in Louisiana.

Nor am I saying that when we are caught, we should be clever, confessing to anyone who will listen—that would be playing another game. I *am* saying that, in a sense, we are *already* caught in whatever we have done. Nobody has to know who we are; no one has to find out; we are already what we are. Let us be introduced to ourselves and stop running away; we should join the human family. Simon Peter knew what he was doing! Surely, he never forgot that he had denied Jesus. He did not talk about it every day of his life, but he started with that experience, accepted it, and lived out of it.

Additionally, let us realize from this story of Peter that *our very weakness can help us to become strong.* Our awareness of that is one of the reasons we appreciate Peter. We say that he is like we are. And when Jesus is pictured with some sense of accuracy, that is one of the things we like about him: We are not as excited by Jesus, the child in the manger, as much as we are drawn to Jesus, the One who in all things was tempted as we are tempted. And remember when he turned to his disciples and said, in words something like these, "Are you going to leave me, too? These other people followed me, but now I am unpopular, and they have gone away. I did not expect everyone to stay with me, but I thought *you* would." Seeing Jesus like that, we can relate to him. He knew what it was to be hurt, to be disappointed, to cry. He was real!

We are slow to learn this lesson—we think that we are worthy and lovable only when we are strong. But we are wrong. A show of strength is often merely a form of bluffing. We find true strength when we put aside pretense and are open and honest. That is when power begins. I am not suggesting that we overconfess our sins, as Luther did. Nor am I suggesting that we do our dirty laundry in public—that would be foolish. But if we are introduced to ourselves as we are, then our very honesty about our weakness helps to make us strong.

That was true in Paul's life, certainly. Probably the greatest statement ever made about love was made by Paul, to the church at Corinth. He was the greatest missionary of all time. But consider his former life. He had changed his name; there was a time when he was known as Saul. It was he who had held the coats of the men who stoned Stephen, that first martyr of the church. What would we think of one of our ministers who played that role?

Paul surely never forgot that experience, but he did not start over again and put the event out of his mind. Rather, he referred to himself as the greatest of sinners. But the gospel takes hold of that sort of man and molds him. So the day came when Paul could write about love. No wonder; he had experienced it! The very thing about ourselves that we despise and hate—the very same weakness that can wreck us—can help to make us strong! I believe that with all my heart.

Finally, a third thing we can learn from the story of Peter is that *we can start where we are because we are accepted, just as we are, by God through Christ.* We are not loved by God in order to make us better, but because of who we are now. When we really like a person, we like that person just as he or she is. Oddly enough, though, our love will make a difference. If the person is ever going to change, our love will help to bring that change about. But we do not love the person *in order* to make that happen. We simply love that person.

God made his world and he never left his world. Jesus was born into this world—that is the Incarnation. God knows us exactly as we are; we need not bluff any longer. God does not play tricks with us by loving us to make us better. However, when we know that, we find that we do become better; we do live beyond our failure. We are loved and accepted as we are. Isn't that preferable to a multitude of new beginnings?

We should be glad that Simon Peter did not start over again. If he had, we might never have known about him. One day he stood up and preached; we call that day Pentecost. Some five thousand people were brought into the fold of the early church. That is powerful preaching! What gave him the power to preach like that? He remembered a night when he had said, "I don't even know the man!" And that weakness, realized and recognized in the light of God's acceptance, helped to heal him. That is far better than trying to wipe out a mistake and pretend that it did not happen. God did that for Peter—and God through Christ can do that with you in your life now.

Anger

CHAPTER II

And he looked around at them with anger, grieved at their hardness of heart, and said to the man, "Stretch out your hand." He stretched it out, and his hand was restored.

—Mark 3:5

So many of us in the church have been taught, either directly or indirectly, that a real conversion includes denying the material and rejecting the flesh. Somehow we have acquired the notion that if we are truly converted, we will find ourselves becoming spiritual and will not have to deal with the worldly. We think our passions and feelings will be under control and that we will always be sweet and placid.

Because of those ideas we find a conflict within ourselves. The reality does not measure up to the expectation. We think that in being converted—being really changed—we will become sweet and good. We want Christ, so we give ourselves over to the conversion, and find ourselves acting, or *trying* to act, passionless and unreal. That is almost a denial of our humanity.

In defending someone we often say, "Well, after all,

he is only human." I should hope so! Wouldn't he look silly if he were totally divine and spiritual? We will never sense the divine for even one fleeting moment in our lives, until we deal honestly with our humanity.

We become whatever feelings we happen to be experiencing at the moment. If we pretend that we do not experience those feelings, and yet we want to know Christ, how is he going to meet us? He cannot meet us while we are pretending to be someone we are not.

I think that Jesus was totally human. He was described as being tempted in the same ways we are tempted. Why did they want to put him to death? They said that he was a wine bibber and a glutton, that he visited with unsavory people, that he was fleshly. But although he was totally human, he did not behave as we do. There was no pretense in Jesus, no affectation. He did not play games. Someone once called him good and he said, "Don't call me good. Only God is good." Jesus was good precisely because he would not accept the guise of goodness. But we are different. We are so intent on playing the divine, or on having God in us and being divine in that manner, that we deny our humanity. Thus, we become artificial.

Let us look at this question of humanity in light of our scripture. Jesus knew the Law. He grew up with it and was trained in it. On this occasion he knew what day it was; it was the sabbath. He was in the synagogue when he became aware of a man with a withered hand. The people around him began to wonder, "What is he going to do now? Will he heal this man on the sabbath? If he does, he will be in trouble with the Law." As often was the case with Jesus, the real question was, Which is the more important thing here, the Law or the human being? So Jesus turned to those gathered around and said, "What is the right thing to do—to take life, or to save life?" The onlookers said nothing. Then Jesus said to the man with the withered hand, "Stretch forth your hand." The man did, and he was healed.

To paraphrase, in the next verse we read, "And the Pharisees went out and made plans to get rid of Jesus, to destroy him." We see ourselves on Jesus' side—against the Law—saying, "Master, you did the right thing in healing this man." We do not think *we* are like those Pharisees were. But we are! That is exactly where we find ourselves—secure and comfortable, insulated from our own humanity, and full of smugness. We do not care enough to become angry in order to change something. But Jesus became angry and was not embarrassed by it. The scripture says clearly, "He looked on them with anger." Some try to explain it by saying it was a holy anger. However, the scripture does not say "holy" anger; it just says "anger."

Anger is a feeling we all experience when we are threatened, when we are thwarted, when we are hurt. Anger comes as a response, as a way of doing something about our predicament. We know anger, but one of our problems is in thinking that we should always be calm and sweet. We see anger only negatively. Yet anger also has a redemptive quality. I doubt seriously if we could love without also experiencing anger. It is a question of our whole involvement in life.

But we have been taught that we are not to admit being angry. A member of the church one day may become angry, and someone might say to him, "You're angry." But because of what he has been taught, he will smile sweetly and say, "Oh no, I'm not!" That is much the same reaction as that of someone who is taking a nap in the afternoon. The telephone rings, he answers, and the person calling asks, "Did I wake you?" And even though the one who answers may still be half asleep, he says, "Oh no, I was just sitting here, waiting for the phone to ring." It embarrasses us to show any kind of irritation, much less anger. But Jesus experienced anger, and so do we, if we are real people.

I think there are basically three types of people, characterized by how they respond to anger. Many psychiatrists say that each of us fits into one of these categories and that we often move from one to another.

The first type is dependent and hates to admit or to show anger, for fear of appearing unlovable. A person who is dependent upon others wants to be loved by others. That person may vent his anger on an object other than its cause; he may release his anger on a harmless target, such as a child who cannot retaliate, or if he is mad at someone in the office, he may go home and kick the dog.

The second way anger is handled is seen in the controlled person. Here is someone who likes to have power and direct other people. For him, anger is not permissible. He has to be perfect, so it is extremely difficult for him to admit that he is either wrong or angry. If we tell a controlled person we are angry with him, he will probably make *us* feel guilty. He will show us that the anger was not his fault. He will convince us that we are overly sensitive. He will say that, if he had done something wrong, he would readily admit it, but that it is not his fault if we wear our feelings on our sleeve.

A third way of dealing with anger is seen in the person who is primarily interested in his self-esteem. Since he has to have the approval of other people, he can never deal with his anger directly; it would make him look bad. If he goes into a rage, he may later say, "Oh, I was only kidding," or "I had a headache." We ought to be glad for headaches! Of course, there are real headaches, but I am referring to those that are excuses. There is a difference between dealing with reality and manufacturing excuses. But who among us does not sometimes say, "Oh, I know what happened, but I wasn't really angry. It was just one of those days!" We do not come to grips with our own emotional reality.

Not dealing with anger has many consequences—some obvious, and some subtle. One obvious result is that we sometimes want to retaliate, rather than deal directly with the problem. That is destructive. Hopefully, that feeling only lasts for a moment. If we are mature, the desire to retaliate begins to go away as soon as we recognize it. But if we do retaliate, what happens? We hurt someone or we ourselves are hurt. If we want to get even with someone, we can become so caught up in trying to do so that it consumes all our energy.

More subtly, anger has hidden consequences. Repression and denial are other destructive methods we employ to avoid dealing directly with anger. These are the methods used by so many of us in the church. We just cover our anger and pretend it is not there. Or, even more destructive, we may not even be aware of our anger because we *have* repressed it. Sometimes when people are very angry, but very religious, all that can be seen of the anger is a smile. They will look very sweet and declare that they did not mean what they said or felt at all. They will say that the world might be angry, but that *they* could never be.

One of the dangers of denial and repression is that they produce fantasy worlds. In one, we live in an angry world, obsessed with spending our anger; in the other, we live in a peaceful world, divorced from reality.

When we deny our anger we live in a world where we dream, ponder, and plot. If you do not believe it, think of someone you do not like. Did you ever wake up in the morning, thinking of that person? You cultivated your dislike and worked on it all day. Maybe that person had not thought about you for six months, but there he was, controlling your life through your fantasy world.

I once heard a story about a man who was driving home late at night. He took a short cut down a dirt road and, on the way, had a flat tire. It was about 1:00 in the morning when he discovered that his jack did not work. Looking down the road, he saw a farmhouse. All the lights were out. He thought that the farmer might have a jack he could borrow, but as he started to walk toward the house he thought, "I'm probably going to make that man mad by knocking at his door at this hour. I'll wake him, and even if he has a jack, he will probably be so furious that he won't let me use it." Finally he reached the farmhouse and knocked on the door. The farmer came to the door, and the motorist shouted, "Keep your old jack!"

We build our fantasy worlds, and we base our actions on them as if they were real.

Despite its negative aspects, there is a place for anger. Real anger can be recognized and used constructively. Its purpose is not the destruction of the world or the injury of people. The purpose of real anger is to make us care enough to become angry. Jesus loved enough to become angry, but you and I direct our anger toward trivialities.

If someone gets in front of us at the supermarket line, we may really get angry about that. But on the other hand, consider that we have lived through the most trying and difficult times in the history of our country.

And what was the church preaching about in the 1950s, the 1960s, and the 1970s? Many of us are white, and middle class. We hold the power. We were comfortable during those years. It was not that we wanted to hurt minorities, but we were so secure in our snug existence that black people had to risk their very lives in order to have the right to sit at a lunch counter. While we were getting angry in supermarket lines, we easily overlooked the crippling aspects of our culture that *should* have made us mad.

We say, "Oh God, I want to be a Christian." If there is such a thing as judgment, why do we not raise our voices about some things that are wrong? We know why. It is because we are so "good" that we do not dare to get angry! We don't love enough to care! That plagues us to this day, not only in race relations, but in almost everything else that is valid. We are inclined to exaggerate petty matters, rather than confront the important issues. We do this so that we can live comfortably in our world. But we ought to care! We ought to love enough to care!

Jesus knew what the people were thinking on that sabbath in the synagogue. The Law said very clearly that one was not to do any kind of work on the sabbath. It was considered work to help a person. One could pull an ox out of a ditch, but one could not help a human being. Now in this situation, obviously, some were waiting to trap him. So what was Jesus going to do? He did not want to rush to the cross; he did not welcome trouble. But his priorities were right—he wanted to bring the Good News to the people. He said, "Stretch forth your hand." The man stretched forth his hand and was healed. The Pharisees immediately went out and planned to destroy Jesus. And he looked on them with anger.

What was Jesus really expressing by his angry look as the Pharisees were about to leave? His meaning was very much like a mother's rebuke to her son. "I am angry because you are so blindly self-righteous and self-destructive that you hurt yourself and other people." A mother would say that to her son and be angry with him, precisely *because* she loved him. If the mother loved him less, she could ignore him. Where did we ever get the idea that anger is the opposite of love? Anger is involved in love! The purpose is not to destroy, but to redeem. Yet, in the church, we are taught to keep our real feelings hidden, because we are supposed to be spiritual. But the way we become spiritual is by dealing with the world—by dealing with our feelings and with ourselves.

Rather than concealing our anger, we should learn to deal with it. And in order to deal with our anger, we must first of all recognize it. When we become angry, we should admit it to ourselves. We should be honest and say, "I'm angry. I don't know if it is justified, but I am mad." We have to recognize our anger. Let us not lie to ourselves just because we are Christians. Let us reverse that and, in the name of common sense, tell ourselves the truth because we *are* Christian and because we are human.

Then we can deal with our anger by expressing the proper response to it. We must not nurture it and let it fester. If someone has hurt us, let us tell that person about it. We should tell him how we feel and how we have responded. That is far better than harboring our anger. If someone asks, "Did I hurt you?" don't say, "Oh, no, it didn't matter at all," when the truth is that it did. We can never be well until we start being honest and dealing with reality; yet many of us are reluctant to do so.

Finally, we ought to deal with our anger because when we do, we are dealing with reality. It is only by dealing with our *real* selves that we can ever find God. As long as we deny our feelings, we will never have the authentic experiences we desire, with God or with people, because we have been fleeing from the real world and trying to find God in make-believe.

If that is difficult to believe, here is an example. Jesus, in his early thirties, walked into the synagogue on a sabbath. Jesus was a real, live, human being. He was conscious of the Law; he was also conscious of a man with a withered hand. "Stretch forth your hand." The man could have lied and said, "What do you mean? There is nothing wrong with my hand." But the man did not deny his disability. He stretched forth his hand and he was healed. If we are going to deal with the issues—if we are going to be honest—let us stretch forth our hands!

Jesus is the model for our dealing realistically and usefully with ourselves. His openness and his anger are our examples. But in his honesty, he is saying more. He is saying, "Show your feelings as they are. Don't lie; don't cover up; don't deceive yourself." There are some things we ought to be angry about. There are things in the world that ought to be made right, and we cannot make them right unless we care enough to struggle with them. Christianity is not a namby-pamby, sweet, and docile life that tranquilizes us. If saying "Walk down the aisle, get your soul saved, and go to heaven" means "That's all there is to it, and we can let the world go to hell," then that is *blasphemy*.

Deal with the real world. Jesus says to us, "Stretch

forth your hand!" We can say, "God, I don't want to; I'm embarrassed. I don't like my feelings. I want people to like me. If they know who I am, they may not care for me." Well, if people do not know who we are, they do not like *us* anyway. They only like what they *think* we are.

We can afford to accept our real feelings. We no longer need to be ashamed of them. Who are we running from? God already knows us! We are not going to make fools of ourselves. While it is true that sometimes we will misuse our anger, we will often use it in the right way. By accepting our feelings as they are, we are recognizing reality—we are becoming more human—and in the process, we are becoming more whole. God was in Christ reconciling the world unto himself. When we dare to allow the Spirit of God to guide us to become real and reveal our true feelings, we may then find the help we need. "Stretch forth your hand!"

Anxiety

CHAPTER III

Then he said to them, "My soul is very sorrowful, even to death; remain here, and watch with me."
—*Matthew 26:38*

Every one of us knows what it is to be anxious. But when is this fear normal? And when is it abnormal?

A person is psychotic when he or she is out of touch with reality; a neurotic person knows what is real. Obviously, the two are not the same. The best definition I know is that a psychotic person thinks two plus two equal five; a neurotic knows that two plus two are four, but he is worried to death about it. That is the difference.

Sometimes anxiety dominates us. We become so frightened that we cannot function, and that is destructive. On the other hand, some of us spend our lives thinking that all fear is bad. We may believe that if we have enough faith we can get rid of our fear—that if we are Christian enough, we will never be anxious. However, I do not think that would be desirable, because the creative part of our lives often comes from a certain tension—a tension created by bringing opposing ideas together. Out of that tension is born growth and change. Yet we have been told that if we are mature enough, we will be tranquil and calm. That may just be another way of saying that we would be dead!

Consider the picture of Jesus in this scripture, at the climax of his ministry. He is about thirty-three years old. He has taught; he has healed; he has loved life; he has loved people. He is so alive! He does not want to die. But he can look at the situation and see that he is not going to change people as he had hoped. He has come into conflict with some people in much the same way that truth comes into conflict with some of us.

Therefore, on the eve of the confrontation and the crucifixion, he went to the Garden of Gethsemane. He took his disciples with him. Then he selected three of them to go further with him, and he left the others behind. Jesus no doubt had faith. And yet he said, "Now is my soul very sorrowful, even unto death." That is being real; that is being honest. "Now is my soul sorrowful." Are those words not filled with anxiety?

Then Jesus left even the three disciples and went away by himself to pray. In effect, he asked, "If it is possible, Father, let this cup pass from me; but if not, and if others are not going to change, let me stay true to my course. And if the cross is the only way I can show people your nature, then, Father, may your will be done through me."

We almost misunderstand this passage. We tend to see Jesus with so much faith that he cannot wait to get to the cross, for he knows that there will be a resurrection. It amazes me that people will read some parts of the Bible so literally, but dilute this portion. The plain truth of the matter is that Jesus did not want to go to the cross—he was frightened! To put his words clearly, "My heart is troubled; my soul is troubled unto death." He behaved as we would have. If we can grasp that, we can begin to grasp the reality of Jesus' fear. Only then can we understand the religious significance.

If we are going to be real people, there is a time when anxiety is normal. But that is not always what we are taught. Instead, we are taught that we are supposed to be perfect. No one may put it to us in those exact words, but we absorb that expectation of ourselves. While we certainly know that we are not, just as surely as others know it, we look at ourselves as if we *ought* to be perfect. For instance, if a student goes to class, and the teacher asks, "Does everyone understand this?" the student may not understand a word of it, but is inclined to keep silent because he does not want to appear dumb. How many times have we said that we understood something, when we did not know the first thing about it? We are just programmed to believe that we are supposed to appear perfect.

We also grow up with the idea that fear is bad and that faith is good. Unfortunately, that theory is preached throughout the church. Yet the truth is that we would not want to live in faith all the time. Is anything more unpleasant than finding someone who always lives in faith? For example, when I have a problem, I sometimes want to talk to someone about it, and I feel I have been brushed aside if that person says, "Oh, just have faith." Probably I did not even have a chance to describe the problem. I wanted to cry a little; I wanted some support. We can go to someone and say, "I think I'm sick and I'm really concerned about it," but before we can even get that much out, they may say with a pious look, "Well, if you have faith, everything will be fine." From the response our fear receives, we learn that fear is bad and that faith is good.

But *without* fear, there *is* no faith. In the classic *Moby Dick,* the captain says, "I will not have anyone on board who is not afraid of a whale!" There are some things in life we *ought* to be afraid of. Try having only faith and see what happens! When we do that, we look like fools. We need to have some sense of discrimination. Faith is not blind. Fear and faith are not enemies.

Just as we are taught to be perfect and fearless, we are also taught to be strong. Little boys, in particular, are taught to be strong and never to cry. What do we think little boys are supposed to do? As an adult, our heart may be broken. It can be obvious that something is troubling us. Yet when someone asks if there is something wrong, we stand there and reply, "No, everything is fine." And then we pat ourselves on the back. How courageous we are! With this kind of pretense, eventually we will not even recognize our own feelings. We think to ourselves, "Be strong!" That really means, "Do not be real—lie!" When we are scared, we pretend we are not.

We are taught another notion that instills guilt in us and produces anxiety. We are taught that thinking of something is the same as doing it. Many people in the church support this notion. We get the idea from the biblical statement that if a man looks upon a woman lustfully, he has already committed adultery with her in his heart. We apply that idea to all things in life, and soon we believe that thinking of anything will make it real. By logical extension of this line of thought, if someone window-shops, looks at a coat, and thinks, "I would like to have that," he might soon begin to think of himself as a thief.

That is how we tend to operate in the church; we instill guilt. Since we are supposed to have faith, but no fear, we do not deal with *any* kind of feeling that might be real or embarrassing to us. We pretend it is not there. Consequently, we suffer from all kinds of anxieties, because we are running from ourselves.

Just as there are some general emotional features that seem to be breeding grounds for anxiety—feelings that we ought to be perfect, that fear is bad, that we are inevitably guilty—there are also some concrete experiences that directly provoke anxiety. For instance, there are times when we become anxious because we are afraid we might lose someone we love. The one we love might leave us, might move away, might stop loving us, might die. That fear creates a certain kind of anxiety in our lives. When we love people, we naturally want to hold on to them. When things are pleasant for us, we want to keep everything as it is, but we cannot do that.

Psychiatrists tell us that there are times when we feel anxiety because our self-esteem is threatened. This is another anxiety-producer. We want to be liked by other people, but we are not really sure that we are. Actually, we do not have a very good self-image. Consider how this process works. If we do not feel good about ourselves unless other people are bragging about us, we need to win their approval. However, that approval does not last very long; even if it is given to us today, we need to win it again tomorrow. We *can* live in that kind of cycle, but it is anxiety-provoking; there is no security. We live under the constant threat of the withdrawal of approval.

A third source of anxiety comes from our fear of losing control of our own lives. But how can we stay in complete control? A change in business, a change in the family—almost anything can threaten our control over events that affect us. Even the most secure person is threatened when he is not calling the shots, for although he may like change, he likes to control the change.

Another cause of anxiety is our fear of our own death. Here, it is not a matter of someone leaving us; it is the fact that *we* are going to die. We do not contemplate our death when we are healthy, but when we are ill, it can become very real. One day we have health and success; the next, illness and the prospect of death. We grow unbearably anxious.

Waiting for a doctor's report can be a time of anxiety. It can be a time when we are frightened to face the fact of our own death, and that is true for every last one of us. That is why, when you are with someone who is afraid, one of the most sacred things you can do is just—*be there*. You don't have to say anything; the other person may just reach out and touch your hand. If we live long enough, such a time—a time when fear is present and very real—comes to every one of us.

So we know what anxieties are. There are these, and more. We are concerned about world events, about the economy, and about how it affects us. We experience world problems, national problems, personal problems. There is no way to eliminate these anxieties we all share. But there *are* some ways to deal with them.

First of all, we should recognize we are scared. We should admit it to someone who is close to us. That is exactly what Jesus did. He asked his disciples to go with him, because he needed them. They went to the garden. He had helped them often with their problems, just as time and again, he had tried to teach them. He had tried to let them know certain secrets of life, so that their lives would be more full. But that is not what he was doing in the garden. There he was saying, "I need you. My soul is troubled even unto death." That is anxiety, is it not?

Therefore, when we are scared to death, let us admit it. In spite of what we may have been taught as children, it is not beneficial to lie about out feelings. Be real! Sometimes that takes courage. And sometimes other people do not want us to admit our fear.

A friend of mine, a minister, was on a plane during a terrible storm. The plane was forced to land before it reached its destination. The passengers waited almost two hours after landing before receiving permission to reboard and continue the flight. My friend and one other passenger were the only ones to reboard the plane; the others decided to wait for better weather.

The plane took off, only to fly into an even worse storm. The other passenger said to the minister, "Buddy, do you mind if I come over and sit by you?" My friend said, "No," so the man sat down and asked, "What do you do?" "I'm a preacher," my friend replied. The man said, "Thank the Lord!" "But," my friend said, "I'm just as scared as you are." (I will omit the man's response.) You see, people often do not want us to admit our fears, but we still should acknowledge them. If we are afraid, we should admit that fact to ourselves.

Second, we should admit our sins to God. We say that Jesus was perfect; we say he had nothing to confess. But he probably never made these claims for himself—we are speaking only from our point of view. But even if he had no sin, I think Jesus would have talked about all those things he had not accomplished. Jesus was in touch with himself and could realize what he had not been able to do. As for ourselves, we *do* need to confess. We are weak; we hurt other people; we hurt ourselves. No wonder we are filled with anxiety—I think we create it! Let us recognize our sins and stop whining and blaming others.

We can confess, because God forgives us—not because we deserve it, not because we are good enough, not because of anything in us. God forgives us because of who *he* is. I am amazed how many times we can admit that we are scared and then do nothing. I do not believe there is any healing apart from religion. This is the confession we need to make: "God, I'm not what I ought to be, and I know it." That is not saying that we are worms; we need not bemoan our plight forever. We simply need to accept the forgiveness God wants to give us.

Third, we can better deal with our anxiety when we accept God's forgiveness, because then we will be living with an awareness of his presence. The fact that we will still be filled with anxiety at times does not mean that we are not Christians. In fact, we are in great company when anxiety comes upon us—the company of one who lived almost two thousand years ago. He was, perhaps, the only truly honest person who has ever lived. With the cross just a short distance away, he said to his disciples, "I want you to come and be with me." That is being honest. Jesus could deal with many situations, but he was not walking on water at that point. He was reaching out for help.

To all of them he said, "Now is my soul sorrowful." There is no pretense in that statement at all. How great it is—filled with anxiety. He turned to three of the disciples and asked them to come with him. He stayed with them for a time; then he went off by himself to be alone with God. And then he prayed. In words we can more easily understand, Jesus said, "Father, if it is possible, let us find a solution to this. If the people can be converted and changed, let us do that. But I must stay on the course that is selected for me and that I have chosen. If there is no way around this—if the only way I can show your love is by the cross—may I be the kind of person your nature can be shown through." This is worded in the scripture, "May thy will be done." And Jesus went to the cross.

It seems to me that Jesus had more faith than anyone else in human history has ever had. But faith, for him, did not mean an absence of fear or anxiety. He had that faith because he was real. Let us recall the last thing he said in his earthly life. "Father, into thy hands I commend my spirit." There are times when we will be frightened and filled with anxiety. There is no way to avoid that, but at those times, let us realize that we are in God's hands. Whatever is troubling us now, or whatever may happen to us later, let us come to that place where we can recognize that we are frightened half to death, and we can truthfully say, "Father, into thy hands I commend my spirit."

Depression

CHAPTER IV

When Judas, his betrayer, saw that he was condemned, he repented and brought back the thirty pieces of silver to the chief priests and the elders, saying, "I have sinned in betraying innocent blood." They said, "What is that to us? See to it yourself." And throwing down the pieces of silver in the temple, he departed; and he went and hanged himself."

—Matthew 27:3-5

It is strange that we in the church seem to convey the idea that after one becomes a Christian, one does not experience any kind of real feeling that might be embarrassing. This can contribute to our becoming artificial, because then we are unable to recognize our true feelings.

Jesus' approach was just the opposite. People felt they could talk to him because he honored their feelings. If they could not talk with other religious persons, they could certainly talk with Jesus. As for those of us who want to be followers of Jesus, we want to appear very religious, so we polish our halos and no one dares talk to us, because they think that we are beyond embarrassing feelings. Jesus dealt with human reality in such a marvelous way, but we have created artificial Christians.

Depression is an embarrassing feeling that we should acknowledge. Contrary to the suggestions of our religion, depression does not mean that we are not Christian, nor does it indicate in any way that we are bad people. Depression is an emotion that we all experience at one time or another, for we all have feelings of unworthiness, unacceptability, and isolation. It is also the kind of emotion that we can produce in ourselves. Two people can go through the same painful experience; one can emerge even stronger, while the other comes out of it in a totally miserable condition. Conversely, when we are depressed, even the most pleasant experience seems only to deepen the depression, as if we deserved nothing good from life. We all know what it is to be depressed, periodically; some of us may think we suffer from chronic depression.

Consider the story of Judas. He had every reason to be depressed. It was toward the end of Jesus' earthly life that Judas betrayed him. But despite the interpretation of this act by the early church, doubtless Judas did not intend for Jesus to be crucified. We like the implication of that part of the story—"For thirty pieces of silver Judas went out and betrayed Jesus"—because then the event seems to be so very clear-cut. We also like having a scapegoat. But I do not believe that Judas expected a crucifixion. If that had been his goal, he would have had a celebration, rather than take his own life. I believe he thought Jesus would resist, would lead an earthly army, would fight back.

Judas did not realize that Jesus was a man who practiced what he preached. Jesus spoke of kindness, but he also embodied it. So at the moment of betrayal,

Jesus turned to Judas and said something like this. "Whatever you are going to do, go ahead and do it quickly. If you've made up you mind, and you really cannot understand me, let's get this over with." So Judas received thirty pieces of silver from the chief priests for identifying Jesus with a kiss, and Jesus was arrested. Of course, Jesus was known and could have been arrested without the help of Judas. Jesus said to the soldiers, "Why did you come like this? You have seen me in the synagogue. You have had many chances to take me." When Judas realized the full significance of what had happened, he went back to the temple and tried to return the money, but no one would take it.

Imagine the plight of Judas at this point: He wanted to undo what had been done. There was Judas, in despair, saying, "Take back the money! I have betrayed innocent blood!" The scripture clearly states, "Judas repented." We have skipped over that phrase. How we have misread the Bible all these years! Judas said, "Here is the money!" When no one would take it, what were his options? He could not return to his friends; the disciples would not have him back. After all, he was evil. Yet, there was something of Judas in each of them. But they could appear so pious! We may assume that we would have done otherwise, but when we are pressured, it becomes obvious how much alike we all are.

Depression is an emotion that engulfs us. When it comes to us as grief and guilt, as unworthiness and despair, to swallow us as it did Judas, we feel there is no way out. Judas did not know there was one place he could have gone. There is always one. We have had two thousand years to reflect and realize this; Judas did not realize it because things were happening so fast. But had he gone to Jesus, although all the disciples had rejected him, Jesus would have accepted him again. I would bet my life on that. I think the greatest Gospel that might have been written, was unwritten, because Judas did not know that Jesus would have taken him back. And not knowing, Judas went out and hanged himself.

There are several qualities that characterize depression. First of all, for many persons, depression is a full-time job. If we want to be really depressed, we need to work at it twenty-four hours a day. We cannot work in the yard, go for a walk, or do anything else, because we must concentrate on our depression, in order to cultivate it. Some of us absolutely exhaust ourselves—as well as those around us—trying to hold onto our depression. It is our identity.

I read some time ago about one of the great leaders of the church, a marvelous old man, who was dying. Someone leaned over his deathbed and asked, "Are you praying now?" "No, I'm not praying now," he replied. "I'm dying now, and I can only do one thing at a time." I love that.

Depression is similar, in that when we are depressed we feel like doing nothing but being depressed. We do not want to sleep. If we eat, we do not enjoy it. When we are depressed, we are caught in an emotion that feeds on itself. Depression can be a full-time job.

I do want to point out that there is all the difference in the world between sorrow and depression. We confuse the two. We all experience feelings of sadness and sorrow. These feelings come for many reasons and, unlike depression, there is usually a clear reason. Our children fail in school, we lose our job, our business does not do as well as it should, we feel rejected, or we get a doctor's report that scares us to death. Whatever the reason, when sorrow or sadness come over us, we can usually identify the source. We can sit back and think, "I know why I feel so terrible."

Should we lose a member of our family or someone we love very much, I think we ought to give ourselves permission to sorrow, and we should anticipate that this process is going to take a long time. If the loss was more than a year ago, and still we do not feel better, we should give ourselves permission to wait longer. We cannot go by the calendar. No matter how strong we are, no matter how much faith and love we have, when we lose someone we love, it takes quite a while to adjust to it. That does not mean that we are weak or unacceptable. It simply means that we are healthy and normal. There are times when we are sad and we can recognize the feeling as sadness.

But depression is different. In depression, we trap the feeling and will not deal with it. Or we deal with the depression, but we will not confront the cause. Depression, many psychiatrists say, stems from anger. If we lose someone we love, we may feel angry because we have been cheated. If there was an accident, we might think, "If that other person had driven more carefully, this would not have happened to my family." Look what has taken place. We have become angry, let us admit it. But nice people are not supposed to be angry; they are supposed to get hurt! Therefore, when we deal with depression, we may manage to say, "I'm sad," but we do not deal with the anger. If our depression results from anger, we will never be able to control our depression until we deal with our anger. Whether or not the anger is justified, does not matter.

Here are four suggestions I think are practical in facing depression. I offer them as ways of dealing with this inevitable experience of life.

First of all, we should recognize that we are not

responsible for anyone else's actions. I know that the church, especially through evangelism, has indicated that we are responsible for saving the world. But we are not. We could not save the world if we tried. We are not even responsible for our own children's actions. We are, however, responsible for ourselves—responsible for being loving, caring people. How others respond to that is up to them, not to us. Jesus loved Judas, but he failed with him. Judas did not understand what Jesus was really saying.

Perhaps we are far too analytical and critical of ourselves. We certainly expect a great deal. We assume that, if we are good parents, we will have marvelous children. That is ridiculous. Some of the finest people we know were almost damned into the world, rather than being born into it, yet they grew up with wonderful attitudes. On the other hand, one may have advantages, privileges, and a wonderful home, and yet grow up uncaring and ingrown. We do not know how to explain these situations.

These facts ought to free us as parents. We are to love our children. We are to love ourselves. We are to care. If someone has a problem, we may be a part of it, but that person decides how he is going to react. We must realize that there is no way on earth we can be responsible for someone else's reactions. There is no way we can be assured that, if we act in the right way, someone else will respond to us in the right way. Judas listened to Jesus for three years. Jesus preached love, and he practiced it, but he lost Judas.

Second, though it has been mentioned before, I want to reemphasize the importance of recognizing our anger, because it is a practical way of dealing with depression. When we get mad, let us admit it. Do not express anger in either an outwardly destructive way, nor more quietly, in manipulative, socially acceptable ways. Just confess it. Until we can deal with our anger, I think we will be locked into our depression.

If we are depressed, the chances are that we are mad at ourselves for doing something, or that we are blaming someone else for making us do something, and that we are mad at them. We are rationalizing and passing the buck. We can simply grovel in our depression. And although we may get over it to a degree, we will never live beyond it, until we acknowledge our anger.

A few years ago I went sailing with some other people on a beautiful river several miles out of Baton Rouge, Louisiana. We sailed for a few hours before going ashore to have dinner with a family who had a cabin on the river. One member of the family was German and a professional chef. Clearly, he was going to be our cook, and he went outside to grill some steaks.

The steaks were waiting on a table while the grill was heating. He and I were talking when, without warning, a dog shot out of nowhere, took one of the steaks and ran off. If you want a helpless feeling, watch a dog run off with a huge steak. And then I heard this man blister the air with German. I never heard the language spoken more rapidly in my life. I asked him what he had said. "Preacher," he replied, "I won't tell you what I said, but I will tell you this much—if that dog spoke German, he'd be dead now!"

He was correct in being angry! Wouldn't he have sounded silly if he had said, "It's all right. Those things will happen," or, "The Lord wants us to feed his animals, so we'll let the dog enjoy the steak."

When irritating incidents like that happen we can handle them, if we will just admit our feelings.

Instead of being angry for a long time, we will probably recover our good nature in a few minutes. We will not stay angry, because we are dealing with the truth. Reality will heal us. The pretense that we like to parade around as Christianity only contributes to our illness.

My third observation about dealing with depression is this: When we are depressed, somewhere along the line, it is helpful to say to ourselves, "I have punished myself long enough." How long do we plan to suffer? Recently I read a book about a woman who was depressed and miserable in her marriage. She felt that she had had enough. Her husband made every decision for her. He told her what to cook, and when, and where, and how. She once served chicken on Monday night, instead of Wednesday, and her husband became enraged. He told her where to have her hair fixed, and how to wear it.

She said she finally woke up one morning and realized that she had made only two decisions in her entire life. The first was to vote for John Kennedy for president, and the second was to name her daughter Jennifer, instead of the name her mother-in-law wanted. At that point, she decided she would not punish herself any longer.

There *is* a way to begin dealing with depression. Why do we keep floundering in it? Do we enjoy the torture? Let us recognize the fact that we have punished ourselves enough.

My last observation about dealing with depression is that ultimately, it is controlled only when we realize that we belong to God. I do not say that because I am a preacher. If I were outside the church, wherever I might be, I would say it, because I believe it. Quite frankly, I cannot see how I could face life without realizing this fact, and I would not want to. I would not want to have so much ability that I would think I could get by on my own. Suppose we did have enough talent to live all by ourselves. How smug and ridiculous we would be. The fact is that we live in God's world. God gives us life. All that we have—even that which we use against God—is a gift of God.

So, fundamentally, we manage depression by realizing that we belong to God, and that we do not have to do one thing in the world to be worthy. We are significant because we are who we are. We are valuable, not because we perform well; we are not dealing with good and bad. That is not the point. We are valuable because we are ourselves. God loves us! God loves us exactly as we are! Should that ever dawn on us, we may be depressed periodically, and we will sometimes experience sadness, but I am here to tell you that we will not be overcome by it!

Now let us return to Judas. All of us know what it is to go out and find darkness. Remember how close Judas was to Jesus, and still Jesus was not able to keep these events from happening. Judas received thirty pieces of silver, and he went over and kissed Jesus. Then he must have realized, "I've betrayed innocent blood. This man isn't going to start an army. He is going to let himself be arrested. They are going to take him to the cross." So Judas tried to return the money. No one would take it. Where could he go? Those disciples would not want him—his guilt would call attention to their guilt. Blame it all on bad Judas—we need a scapegoat. Why, he has tried to go to the priests, but even they would not accept his money.

So Judas threw the money on the floor and walked out. It was night, and he hanged himself. If Judas had only known—and this applies to all modern Judases—if Judas had only known that there was one to whom he could go, I am convinced that the greatest Gospel in all the world—in all the Bible—would have been written. It would call us back from the failure and defeat of our depressions.

On the first day after the resurrection, Jesus turned to the people saying, "Go tell my disciples and Peter to meet me in Jerusalem." He said "Peter," for he knew Peter would not call himself a disciple any longer, because he had denied Jesus. He would have said the same to Judas.

This means that the farther out we think we are, the more we think we need a special invitation. For instance, if I do not think you like me, though you say you want everyone to come to your party, I will not feel you really want me. So if you actually do want me, you are aware of my feeling, and you invite me personally. The farther away from God we are, the more we need a special invitaton. Jesus knew that. "Go tell my disciples," would not be enough. Jesus was thinking, "Simon Peter won't even think he is a disciple, because he has denied me." So he said, "Go tell my disciples and Peter to meet me in Jerusalem."

If Judas had known how much Jesus loved him, we would have a Gospel that we simply could not contain in our minds, because I think it would read, "Go and tell my disciples and Peter and Judas to meet me in Jerusalem." That is exactly what God through Jesus Christ says to you and to me. "Go and tell them to come and be with me now." No matter how depressed we are, we should wrestle with it, and beyond our efforts, the grace of God through Christ will meet us where we struggle. Do not be ashamed. The grace and love of God will heal our depression. It is a fact. If you do not believe it, why don't you try it?

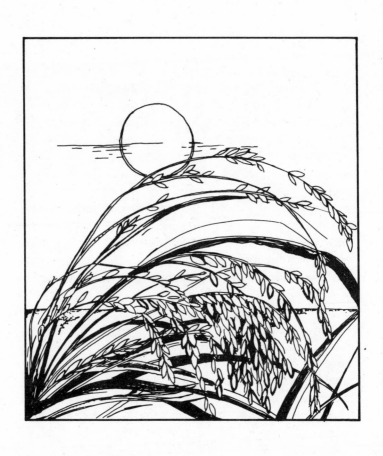

Guilt

CHAPTER V

*I will arise and go to my father, and I will say to him,
"Father, I have sinned against heaven and before you; I
am no longer worthy to be called your son; treat me as one
of your hired servants." And he arose and came to his
father. But while he was yet at a distance, his father saw
him and had compasson, and ran and embraced him and
kissed him. And the son said to him, "Father, I have
sinned against heaven and before you; I am no longer
worthy to be called your son." But the father said to his
servants, "Bring quickly the best robe, and put it on him;
and put a ring on his hand, and shoes on his feet; and
bring the fatted calf and kill it, and let us eat and make
merry; for this my son was dead, and is alive again; he
was lost, and is found." And they began to make merry.*
—Luke 15:18-24

Guilt by itself is destructive, and of no use whatso-
ever. And unfortunately, those of us in the church
certainly know how to feel guilty. All of us have heard
many sermons about guilt, and through these sermons,
the church has tried to tell us that we need forgiveness.
That is true, of course, but remember that Jesus never

forced guilt on anybody. In fact, he did just the opposite.

When we know we are wrong, we have already punished ourselves enough. It is then time to get up and walk—to open our eyes—to reach for the forgiveness of God.

We do not read very far into the Bible before we meet people who are involved in guilt. We find Adam and Eve in the garden, trying to make up their own rules. That is also our hope and our dismay. Science moves forward because someone says we can go on and stretch things beyond our limit. But that same overreach can destroy us, for we can decide that we do not really need anyone else, if we can create everything we require. Adam and Eve finally felt guilty about what they had done and became so wrapped up in their guilt that they hid from God. Adam blamed Eve; Eve blamed the serpent. The buck was passed, but the guilt remained. We behave exactly as Adam and Eve did. Their story is far more true than much of what we call fact, because it describes human nature.

In his guilt, Adam tried to run from himself, and then he felt God speak to him, asking, "Where art thou, Adam?" In response to God's question, Adam replied, "I was afraid and tried to hide myself." That is exactly the way we act. We do what we should not do, and then we become caught up in our own guilt and evict ourselves from the garden. We do not know how to appreciate something until it is threatened or taken away. "I was afraid and tried to hide myself."

If the story of Adam and Eve says something about being caught up in guilt, the story of the prodigal son says something about freedom from guilt. One day a son turned to his father and said, "Give me what is mine." What he referred to as his, was his because his father had given it to him; it was a gift, an inheritance. It is as if we said to God, "God, give me what is mine—my life." Our lives are gifts from God. All the things we love and treasure have been given to us by God, regardless of how hard we might have worked for them.

So the prodigal son took what was his, as we do. We take what is ours, pollute it, tarnish it, corrupt it. Sometimes we do this in a very dignified, socially acceptable way. But, still, in so doing, we hurt ourselves and others.

In dire straits in a far country, the prodigal son began to "come to himself." He thought, "How many servants of my father have bread enough and to spare?" Stretched to his limits, the son says, in effect, "I'm going back home and be honest. I have sinned before heaven and in my father's sight. I will arise and go to my father." And that is just what he did.

He could have stayed and wallowed in his guilt forever. But that would have been destructive, in the way that Adam and Eve's guilty hiddenness was destructive. And that would have been less than honest. Though he could have moaned and he could have gotten up every day to repent again—which would have appeared very religious to many of us—the prodigal did not.

Yet it seems that the church sometimes wants people to wallow, to moan and groan. The church sometimes overplays its hand. The church is to bring us the Good News; it is to heal us. But we sometimes have the notion that we want to be sure that all those in the church, and outside it, know that they are sinners. After all, they are guilty, and we had better let them know it and call them to repentance.

What aggravates the problem further is the fact that so

many people *love* to feel guilty. There are some people who *need* to have a preacher heap guilt upon them. Then they feel so righteous and religious that they do not have to do anything about their guilt themselves. If I come into the pulpit and criticize you it makes you feel spiritual, but you do not have to change. I chastise you, and you say, "He really did a good job today!" But then you go right on doing whatever you were doing.

The church has been successful in helping to make us feel guilty, because the truth is that we do not measure up. Any preacher could tell us that. We all sin. We are not as good as we ought to be, and we are never going to be as good as we hope to be. The gospel is so good, that by comparison, when we consider all our failings, we are like pygmies. If that cannot make us feel guilty, what can? The church reminds us of that so often that we feel we are only getting what we deserve.

But the prodigal son had no one to preach to him, and he did not preach to himself, bemoaning his guilt. Instead, he did a healthy thing—he simply admitted that he had sinned! He did not beat his breast, but went back to see his father—he did something concrete about his repentance. Many of us work so hard on our guilt that we may never get well—we may never correct the problem that brought about our guilt.

One of the organizations that I most admire is Alcoholics Anonymous. When someone has a drinking problem, he or she often feels guilty. I never knew an alcoholic who did not feel guilty about his drinking. He may swear off the bottle and be determined not to take a drink, but he is more likely to take one before the day is over, if he is feeling guilty. He feels unworthy—he feels outside the human family. He thinks, "Look what I have done with my life, to my family, with my money." As long as he feels guilty, he has to drink in order to tolerate the guilt.

Ah, but there is an answer to this problem, and there are thousands of men and women who can testify to it. One day they push through their guilt and deal with reality. They face their problems head on and address the problems, rather than the guilt. Where did we ever get the idea that Christianity is supposed to make us feel guilty? Though that may be what we have been taught, Christianity is there to help us push beyond guilt.

In dealing with the idea of guilt, there are several things we ought to recognize. First of all, we need to see the difference between real guilt and a false sense of guilt. Perhaps this false sense of guilt, which we all experience to some degree, stems from our backgrounds or from our personalities. It makes us feel guilty for simply being. We feel guilty when we fail, and we feel guilty when we do well, because we think we do not deserve it.

Now, there are problems in our world that are absolutely overwhelming—hunger, for example. I suppose that, if every time we sat down to a meal, we could actually see the hungry people in Calcutta, we could not eat a bite. But we eat daily, knowing that there are starving people in Calcutta, yet being unaware of them. We know they live like animals, hoping to find a garbage can with some scraps of food. Although we did not create their hunger, we *are* part of the world which produces such despair. For me to say that I have nothing to do with this hunger is irresponsible, because in order to exist, I am in some way taking away from another. But to dwell on these thoughts can make us neurotic.

We should give ourselves permission to be aware of the sins of the world, as well as permission to be aware of our social sins. Yet we must see that we did not *cause* the sins of the world, nor is it appropriate for us to feel guilty about them. But that guilt is instilled into many of us. It is a guilt that makes us want to apologize for breathing, for being. It is not an honest guilt. It is destructive.

But there is also real guilt. There are times when we *do* hurt other people, as well as ourselves. We do not know how to explain it, but we do these things periodically. We have hurt someone's feelings, or we were less than we should have been, and we are aware of it. When that happens, let us deal not only with the guilt, but with the issue. Better to deal with what has provoked the guilt than to live with the guilt.

Several weeks ago I did something I have never done before and hope never to do again: I forgot a wedding! The wedding was scheduled for a Saturday night in the chapel. I had been working on my sermon most of the day and felt it was going pretty well, so I thought I would leave it and do some visiting. I put on sport clothes and looked as nonclerical as possible.

I was enjoying the prospect of seeing some people who had asked me to come by, but when I made the first stop, I was met at the door with a message from the church. The janitor had left word that a wedding party was waiting for me. They had been waiting for thirty minutes, and the chapel was full.

Arriving at the church, I did not have time to change clothes, so I put on a robe and an academic hood, to hide the fact that I was not wearing a tie. I felt embarrassed, and I left as soon as the wedding was over. The next day someone called and said, "You left so quickly!" "I did not want anyone to realize that I wasn't wearing a tie!" I replied. "Barry, he said, "Everyone there knew you weren't wearing a tie!" When something like that happens, what do you do? You wait long enough, and then confess it in print!

Sometimes we do things that are embarrassing. At other times, we do things that are devastating. We can tear our lives apart. There is no laughter then—it may hurt beyond our ability to express. We do not know why we do these things. We cannot accurately explain why we did the worst thing we ever did in our lives. Chances are it was something we promised ourselves we would never do, and we feel guilty about it. That is real guilt; it is obvious and identifiable.

But Jesus never made anyone feel guilty. Notice what happened when the prodigal son came home. His father did not rebuke him by saying, "You wasted my money! I'm embarrassed in front of the neighbors. Look at all the problems you have caused!" Instead, the father ran and fell on his son's neck and kissed him. If we can agree on anything about parenting, we can agree that one of the most destructive things a parent can say to a child is, "If you do not do what I want I will not love you any longer." *That* is destructive.

And if that would be destructive for a parent to say to a child, think about this carefully: How does it sound to you to be told that is the way God deals with us? If you do not measure up, God will not love you. That is what we have been told, but that is not what we read in the teachings of Jesus. What did the prodigal son deserve? He had wasted his life, but he said he was going home to face the truth. And at home he found a father ready to forgive, not to condemn.

If we are not careful, the Bible, misunderstood, can instill guilt in us at the very time we seek healing. The guilt will make us feel all the more unworthy, thus driving us further into our sin. As long as we feel guilty, we are not likely to change. Our feeling of guilt draws us closer to every kind of weakness in our lives; it does not encourage us to become better.

From this story of the prodigal son, and from our experience, I think there are three things we can conclude that will help us in dealing with guilt.

First, we need to try to be totally honest with ourselves. Let us try to deal with the real issues. If we hurt someone, we need to feel guilty about it just long enough to know that we have hurt them. At that point, we should deal with the hurt, and not with the guilt. If someone is going to put out a fire, he does not work on the smoke. Rather, he puts the water where the fire is. Guilt is like the smoke: it distracts us from the issue. Be honest about the issue.

Second, we need to ask ourselves what we really want. Do we want to be guilty, or do we want to improve? What are we afraid of? If someone knows us for what we really are, are we afraid he will not like us? Are we afraid of being caught? Are we afraid that if we look at the truth about our lives, we will not like ourselves? We ought to sit down and ask, "What are we working for? Is it to impress other people?" If so, we can never impress them enough; they cannot boast about us enough to make us feel secure. What do we really want our lives to become? The more we feel our guilt, the more sick we become. If we do not like ourselves, how can we really care for someone else?

Guilt makes a hell of our lives. There are times when we need to feel guilty, but then let us deal with the real issue, rather than with the guilt.

I do not remember that my parents ever made me feel guilty. They did work at trying to help me be responsible. I remember one day when I was a teen-ager, and my father and I were checking some telephone lines. He was trying to determine a trouble spot, while I was driving the car. We were on a gravel road, when suddenly, I found that I had driven off the road into a ditch. The car seemed about to turn over; it rocked from side to side while the two of us sat there. I felt so foolish! My father turned to me and asked, "What are you going to do?" "I'm going to get out," I replied. "I want you to drive." He said, "Not at all. You can drive this car. Sit there until you feel better and then go on and drive." That was it. I do not remember his mentioning this incident again, nor did anyone else ever remind me of it.

Would you like to know how a preacher would handle a thing like that? If my son had been driving, the accident would have provided the opportunity for a sermon. I would hate to pass up a good opportunity like that! It would be easy to say something like, "Look what you have done! I give you an 'A' in ditch, but you failed the road!"

To my knowledge, my father never read a book on psychology in his life. But I was encouraged to be honest with him because he was who he was. I often found myself looking back at my life and telling my parents things about myself. That is what the prodigal son did. He returned and said, "I have ruined my life. I have sinned before heaven and in your sight. I am embarrassed." There was one person to whom the prodigal knew he could return. That person was not going to cover him with guilt. That person would deal with him lovingly and realistically. "I will arise and go to my father."

Finally, just as it is important to be honest and to choose to push beyond guilt, if we are to avoid its destructiveness, it is also important for us to accept and to appreciate ourselves. In fact, one response to guilt lies in our arriving at the point where we try to please ourselves. That may sound selfish, but it is basic Christianity. If we spend our lives trying to please other people, we will become cynical and disillusioned, because they will not give us the recognition we think we need.

Let us start with "The kingdom of God is within you." And also remember to love our neighbor as we love ourselves. Let us live for ourselves. That is not selfish, for in so living we can live for God and for other people, because the real self within us wants to be good. We *want* to be loving people. The real self within us is like an idea waiting to be born, to burst forth. It is *beyond* what we are!

Peter Nero, the pianist, was in Fort Worth recently to play a concert with the symphony orchestra. Late in the afternoon on the day before the concert, Mr. Nero called the church. He asked if he could practice on one of our pianos. Now I have been a fan of his for years, and I quickly said that he could have every piano we had, plus the organ, and whatever else he wanted. I picked him up, brought him to the church, and he gave a private "concert" for about forty-five minutes. It was perfectly delightful.

Afterwards, we visited for awhile. He said several things that interested me, but one thing, in particular, stood out. Mr. Nero has been recording since 1961, but he did not receive his first gold record until 1972. I asked him if he had any idea why that was so. He said, "The difference was in my playing, and I think I know what it was. I began to play for *myself,* my true self, and then I invited the audience to join me and listen."

That is the way to live. Let the kingdom of God be

within us. Who on earth should we please, more than ourselves? We are sacred. When we do a good job of living for ourselves, we will like ourselves. We will not become selfish. For the first time in our lives, we will be more generous; we will love other people more than we ever have, because we like ourselves. That is why Jesus had no guilty feelings. He loved life to the extent that he loved himself. He loved God. So he naturally loved other people.

We have been taught for a long time that we are supposed to be doormats. We are supposed to spend our lives taking care of others; and when we do not do that, we feel guilty about it. Let us turn that around. God made us and he has given us a gift—he has given us ourselves. We should be thankful for that. We do not need to be anyone else—we can be ourselves! Surely, we will commit sins; we will do things that are wrong; we will feel guilty. But we should deal with the underlying issue and not just with the guilty feeling.

So the prodigal son "came to himself." In recognizing his sin, he was dealing realistically with his guilt. When he was still a great way off, his father saw him, ran to him, kissed him, and said, "My son is alive and home again."

In the end, there are those things you ought to feel guilty about. When that is true, recognize them, but then push the guilt aside and deal with the issue. Accept the love of God in the midst of your guilt. Then you may be surprised how much you will like yourself, because you will realize that you are loved by God. Guilt does not bind you any longer. Then you can stand up, go home, and meet your Father.

Free to Be Human

CHAPTER VI

And God spoke all these words, saying, "I am the Lord your God, who brought you out of the land of Egypt, out of the house of bondage. You shall have no other gods before me."

—Exodus 20:1-3

Our understanding of God is vital because the way we see God affects the way we are. I am well aware that people sometimes have a very poor theology, yet they are very wonderful people. And sometimes people have a healthy theology, but they do not allow it to show in their lives. But as a society and as a world, we will not make much progress in terms of growth and responsibility in sensitive issues until our understanding of God improves. Therefore, it is imperative that we deal with the nature of God.

Basically, the question is very clear. It is not, Do you believe in God? but, What kind of God do you believe in? Jesus spent his life, his teachings, his whole ministry, to one end—the development of our understanding of God.

In Genesis, we read that God is Creator. That is how

we meet God, and that is all that we know of him for a while. "God made everything that was made." That is a marvelous thought. We read it; we will never outgrow it; we must always be aware of it. But that is not the whole picture. God brought the entire world into being, and then he brought each of us into being. Furthermore, he is still creating the world. We should never consider this creation solely in the past tense. God is even now in the process of creating and will be creating his world tomorrow and through all the days that follow.

Reading in the Old Testament through Genesis, we also discover that God is a delivering God. In the book of Exodus we read, "I brought you out of the land of Egypt. I brought you out of bondage." That is the theme of Jewish history. Whenever a rabbi deals with something basic in Jewish history, he will often begin, "Hear, O Israel, I brought you out of Egypt. I brought you out of bondage."

There are times when we need to remind ourselves that God can bring us out of bondage. I can view God in a way that leads me to think of him primarily as loving and kind, for that is easy to see. When my life is rather comfortable and my work is going well, I can assume that God is in his heaven and that all is right with the world. But there comes a time when I need something more personal. I need a God who delivers.

If we know someone lying sick in a hospital, we are frightened because we do not know whether that person will get well. Then we need a God who heals and delivers. Or if the person should not get well, we need the presence of God even more, to be with us in that time of loss and despair. At that point, we do not read about the history of Israel as something that happened very long ago. We feel as though *we* are Israel, and we need his word to come to us—"I brought you out of bondage." Doesn't each of us at some time have an Egypt from which we need to be freed? We have all been in Egypt symbolically, caught in our own defeatism and lostness. How long will we wander in the wilderness?

When we read the history of the Jewish people, we read on two levels at the same time—the past and the present—they were brought out of bondage, and so are we. But let us read on in this story. The day came when God was introduced by the prophets in yet another way. The Israelites finally moved out of bondage and into their land of milk and honey, but they were not allowed to live there long. It was not that God took it away from them; rather, they lost it, and then they were carried into exile in foreign lands.

But that is not the end, for the prophets began to speak. In a way, this is the greatest era of Jewish history. The prophets introduced the idea of ethics, morality, a deeper meaning of the worship of God, the truer essence of God. One of the greatest prophets of all summed it up. "What does the Lord require of you, but to do justice, to love mercy, and to walk humbly with your God?" That is what God is like. We see God as Creator, we see God as Deliverer, we see God concerned with the ethical. If we follow this thought, we see that Jesus stepped into an established line of tradition.

There is a special aspect of that long line of tradition that we must take into account in considering how Jesus showed us God. This is the aspect of sacrifice. We find in Jewish history the belief that it was necessary to sacrifice to God. Their idea was very clear: God made us, we sinned, and the only way we can again become acceptable to God is by making a sacrifice. There was a time when human sacrifices were made. We find allusions to this not only in Hebrew history, but in numerous other religions. If we really want God to accept us, we offer him what is dearest to us. "What do the gods require of us?" This is what the people of the world have asked. We find an element of this sacrifice in the story of Abraham and Isaac.

Doesn't this idea make sense? If we assume that God made us and that he is jealous, and if we sin, and he is angry, and we want him to take us back, we must offer something to appease him. Is that not how people get *us* in a good humor? If you are the boss and someone makes you angry, he brings you a present to get back in your good graces. Isn't that the way we deal with one another? Although we never cease trying to believe that God is like we are, God's ways are not our ways. Nonetheless, human sacrifice was offered.

Eventually, the Hebrew people grew beyond this and began to offer animal sacrifice. That was the pattern for a long time. We would have seen the blood flow freely if we had been in Jerusalem on one of the high holy days. Hundreds of animals were sacrificed at the altar for this one reason: They offered to God what was dear to them, in order to regain his acceptance.

Into this tradition Jesus was born. And this is the subtle part—it is where some of you will disagree with me. Of course, you have every right to do so. But whether you are in accord with me or not, you will notice that we, as Christians, really never changed our idea of God, and that is how we trap ourselves. Jesus came, lived, taught, and showed us God in a way no one had before, yet he was crucified. Then men began to say, "We know why he was crucified. It was to get God to take us back. His blood was shed for us. Never again will we have to offer another sacrifice." I disagree with that interpretation.

Jesus' blood saves us, but in a different way. His life saves us, but in a different way. What some have here is an idea that results in a good Jesus and a bad God. Jesus came to show us God, but I do not believe that God wanted Jesus to die. Men killed Jesus! God and Jesus are alike—caring and divine—but we didn't accept it then, and we don't always accept it now.

And I do not believe that Jesus wanted to die. He was in the Garden of Gethsemane on Thursday, his last night, and prayed, "God, if it is possible, let this cup pass from me, but, nevertheless, not my will but thine be done." We misinterpret that passage by reading it as if God's mind was made up, and he wanted Jesus to go to the cross. If that were the case, God did it. If that were his will—to crucify his own son—we need not repent.

Let us stop and think. If a prophet, long before Jesus, could say that God requires of us only that we love mercy, do justice, and walk humbly with our God, how long must we live as Christians before we begin to realize that? I want to say this as clearly as I can: We have misinterpreted Christianity at this crucial point. I do not see how we can ever have a better understanding of God until we perceive what Jesus came to teach us. In Christianity, we have developed the idea of a good Jesus and a bad God. We have taken the message of Jesus and warped it. We say that God demanded that Jesus die. That is *not* right! Learn from what Jesus said. "He who has seen me has seen the Father." When we see Jesus, we see God. Jesus did not require that anyone should be hurt, and if Jesus is like God, then God did not require such a thing.

Listen to the prayer in the garden again. Jesus is

really saying, "O God, if it is possible, let us find some way around this." He wanted to teach, to live, to love. "But, O God, if they are determined to do what their minds are leaning toward, they will do away with me. Give me the strength to show them your love, regardless." Then, later, to his accusers, Jesus said, in effect, "No one makes me do this thing. Now that your minds are made up, I'll walk to my cross." And on the cross he hung and showed us . . . God! For when he said, "Father, forgive them, they know not what they do," it was God who was praying. We couldn't hear what God was saying, so Jesus expressed it. God was saying that he loves us. That eternal message comes from the cross.

God is our friend. He is good. He is not going to destroy his world. Somehow this is often hidden from us. For some reason, many of us imagine God as a petty dictator who is austere, demanding, and cruel. We can think that he would say to us, "I have made you, and if you sin enough, I will send you to hell. If you displease me even a little, I will mark you off. You had better have faith in Jesus, and you had better have the right answers and do what you should, or you will be consigned to hell forever."

Do we not realize that if God is totally love, he could not enjoy heaven if anyone is outside it? Think of it this way. You are a good parent, and you consider yourself a fairly good person. If one of *your* children were in agony, and you knew it, could you lead a peaceful life? Impossible! And God is at least as good as we are! How could he celebrate heaven if one of his children were in hell? God is not going to destroy his world! God loves us!

Nevertheless, some people seem to relish what they

see as the wrath and destructiveness of God. Their God is full of retribution. What is more, these people often cling to the book of Revelation, misreading it, I think, and gleefully announce that, compared to the wrath to come, we have seen nothing yet!

The book of Revelation is not a book of predictions about airplanes, rubber tires, and the end of the world. It is not that at all! That book barely got into the Bible; it was allowed to slip in. But if it is one of your favorite books, go ahead and read it. If it helps you to know God better, learn from it. But in the name of common sense, do not go running around trying to make everybody else a nervous wreck! God is not going to destroy his world. I wish I could come back a thousand years from now and say, "See, I told you so! It didn't happen."

No, God is not like that. But there are some people who have to be frightened into taking things seriously—for instance, a man who will not kiss his wife unless he thinks she is dying; or a man who will not work at his job unless he is about to be fired; or a student who will not study until he is about to fail. Some people will not think about God unless they believe the world is coming to an end. If you are like that, that is *your* problem. If the only way we are going to get our houses in order is to think that everything is coming to a dead end now, we are viewing God in the wrong way.

But suppose God were a destructive, vengeful deity? What kind of God would we have? Personally, I would rather go to hell believing in the idea of God that Jesus taught, than to get into the kind of heaven suggested by such a vengeful God. Many people feel the same, but from the time they were children, they have been taught the wrong understanding of God. Yet, who would want to treat people the way that angry God does? God is good. Let us permit God to be better than we are.

We should also remember that there is judgment, but it comes through grace and love. A good teacher fails a little bit, too, when he or she has to fail a student. God's judgment is almost like a sign that directs us back to the right road. It is not that God happily catches us in a trap and punishes us. That is something *we* would do. God is good, and when there is judgment, it comes through his love and grace.

When I was growing up in Sheridan, Arkansas, there were two or three ministers who thought I ought to go into the ministry. Truthfully, preaching was about the only thing I knew I did not want to do with my life. However, when I was about twelve years old, one day my own minister invited me to go to Little Rock with him and his wife. He and I stayed together, and his wife was to meet us at the car at a certain time. She arrived two hours late.

I was sitting in the car with him, waiting. It was before the days of air conditioning, and we ran out of things to talk about. I wondered what the preacher would say to his wife when she finally got back. I thought, when she shows up, if he says, "Dear, I have been in prayer all the time you were away, and I'm so glad the Lord returned you to me," I would be nauseated. But when she returned, he was angry. I do not mean that he threw a fit all the way home—only part of the way. He complained angrily, "Why did you do this to us?" He did not try to impress me with his sweetness. He was real. He judged her, but he loved her. Life ought to be like that. God is like that.

God does not say, "Live any way you want, and I will make it all right," for when we damage ourselves, we break God's heart. And then God gets in there with us and helps us remold our lives. God does not sit far away in some distant heaven and point a finger at us and say, "Forget it! I told you how to act, and you ruined yourself. Now, pay for it forever!" No—when we hurt, God hurts.

God is good. God judges us, but that should not scare us. God judges us with his grace, like a doctor who cares. He comes to us in order to help us get well. We are not frightened when the doctor comes in the door. We have been waiting for him. He may have to bring us bad news, but we would rather hear it from him than from anyone else. And the bad news he brings may also give us hope. That is how God works with us and judges us.

Yet that is not what we have been taught. People have worked on us to get our money. They have scared hell out of us to try to make us loyal to the church. They have played on our fear of God's judgment, and they have overlooked his grace. But that is not what Jesus taught, and his whole life was lived to show us God.

Clearly, God wants life for us and judges us graciously. Beyond that, we may grow to understand that it is by God's love that we are saved. God loves us and *that* is what is going to save us. God loves us as we are. He loves us even in our sin. Some of us may not want to hear that. God loves us in our temper, in our badness, in our innermost desires. God moves into our sin with us. Frankly, if he does not move into it, how is he going to save us?

How do we know that to be true? We know it to be true because that is what Jesus taught, lived, and revealed. We are saved by Jesus, who hung on a cross and said, "As I love you, God loves you." That said it all, didn't it? There is no barrier between us and God, though we did not know that, before the cross. But we had trouble accepting that fact, and so we raised another barrier by making Jesus the sacrificial lamb that buys off God. That is not the way God is!

Ultimately, the question is not, Do we believe in God? but, What kind of God do we believe in? We will never know all the truth, but we can know a great deal. We can know God as Creator and Sustainer. We can know him as Deliverer in our personal exodus. We can know him as Judge. And, through Jesus, we can know him most fully as Good and as Love. God loves you. That will convert you, change you, save you—not because of how good you may ever become, but because of what God is!